Animaths

Adding with Ants

Tracey Steffora

Rai

Raintree is an imprint of Capstone Global Library Limited, a company incorporated in England and Wales having its registered office at 7 Pilgrim Street, London, EC4V 6LB – Registered company number: 6695582

www.raintreepublishers.co.uk
myorders@raintreepublishers.co.uk

Text © Capstone Global Library Limited 2014
First published in hardback in 2014
First published in paperback in 2015

Edited by Daniel Nunn, Abby Colich, and Sian Smith
Designed by Joanna Hinton-Malivoire
Picture research by Elizabeth Alexander
Production by Victoria Fitzgerald
Originated by Capstone Global Library Ltd
Printed and bound in China by Leo Paper Products Ltd

ISBN 978 1 4062 6049 6 (hardback)
17 16 15 14 13
10 9 8 7 6 5 4 3 2 1

ISBN 978 1 4062 6056 4 (paperback)
18 17 16 15 14
10 9 8 7 6 5 4 3 2 1

British Library Cataloguing in Publication Data
A full catalogue record for this book is available from the British Library.

Acknowledgements
We would like to thank the following for permission to reproduce photographs: iStockphoto pp.12, 19 (© arlindo71); Photoshot p.22 (A.N.T. Photo Library/ NHPA); Shutterstock pp. 4 (© Micha Klootwijk), 5 (© Mike VON BERGEN), 6, 7, 9 (© Eric Isselee), 8,9,10,11,13,15 (© Potapov Alexander, © Andrey Pavlov), 14, 15 (© Evgeniy Ayupov), 14, 15, 17, 19, 20 (© jps), 14, 15, 17 (© asharkyu).

Front and back cover photographs of forest ants reproduced with permission of Shutterstock (© Potapov Alexander). Front cover photograph of ants on grass reproduced with permission of Shutterstock (© Andrey Armyagov).

We would like to thank Elaine Bennett for her invaluable help in the preparation of this book.

Every effort has been made to contact copyright holders of material reproduced in this book. Any omissions will be rectified in subsequent printings if notice is given to the publisher.

Contents

Some words are shown in bold, **like this**. You can find them in a glossary on page 23.

Adding with ants

Look at this leaf cutter ant. It is carrying a leaf!

Ants work together as a group. When we want to know how many there are all together in a group, we can **add** to find out. Let's add some ants!

Counting all ants

One ant carries a leaf.

Here come two more ants.

1   **2**   **3**

Here are all the ants. How many are there altogether? Count and find out.

We can **add** to find out how many there are altogether.

One **plus** two is three.

There are three ants altogether.

1 + 2 = 3

Double the ants!

Three ants are marching to the nest.

Along come three more! How many
are there altogether?

$$3 + 3 = ?$$

Start with three ants.

Add three more.

Three **plus** three is six.

$$3 + 3 = 6$$

There are **double** the ants!

Counting on ants

Six ants are marching through the forest.

Along come three more! How many are there altogether?

We can **add** by counting on.

Start with six ants.

Count on three more.

$$6 + 3 = ?$$

Six **plus** three **equals** nine. There are nine ants altogether.

Counting on is a fast way to find out how many there are altogether.

6 + 3 = 9

Look! There are two ants on an **anthill**.

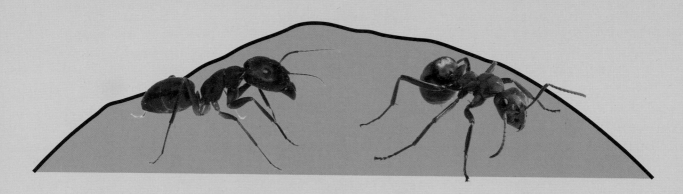

Now five ants are marching along to join them. How many are there altogether?

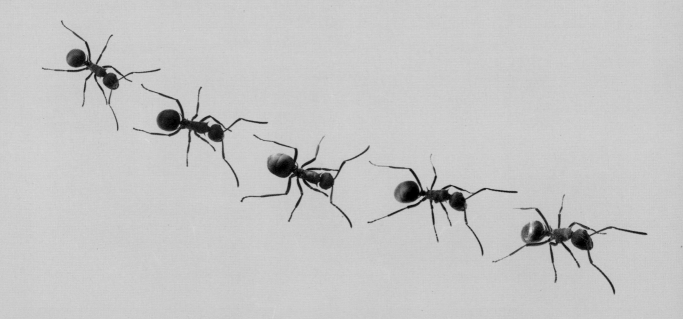

Start with two. Count on five times.

Two **plus** five **equals** seven.

2 + 5 = 7

We can **add** up numbers in any order.

Two **plus** five is seven.

$$2 + 5 = 7$$

Five plus two is also seven!

$$5 + 2 = 7$$

It is easier to count on when we start with the biggest number.

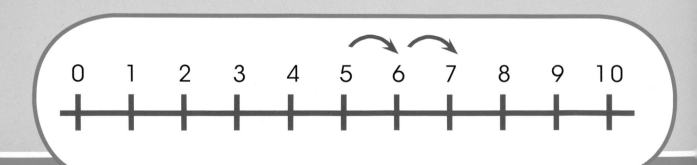

The nine ants in the forest keep marching along.

They join together with the seven ants on the **anthill**.

Now how many are there?

9 + 7 = ?

Nine **plus** seven **equals** sixteen. There
are sixteen ants in total.

$$9 + 7 = 16$$

0 1 2 3 4 5 6 7 8 9 10 11 12 13 14 15 16 17 18 19 20

Count on seven.

Start with nine.

Sixteen ants! That is a **colony** of ants going into the nest!

Addition chart

Look at the pattern of numbers on this chart. It can help us to **add** numbers.

Let's try it together. $6 + 3 = ?$

0	1	2	3	4	5	6	7	8	9
1	2	3	4	5	6	7	8	9	10
2	3	4	5	6	7	8	9	10	11
3	4	5	6	7	8	9	10	11	12
4	5	6	7	8	9	10	11	12	13
5	6	7	8	9	10	11	12	13	14
6	7	8	9	10	11	12	13	14	15
7	8	9	10	11	12	13	14	15	16
8	9	10	11	12	13	14	15	16	17
9	10	11	12	13	14	15	16	17	18

Put one finger on the red six.

Put the other finger on the blue three.

Slide your fingers until they meet.

Now it's your turn!

What is seven **plus** four?

Put one finger on the red seven.

Put the other finger on the blue four.

Slide your fingers until they meet.

7 + 4 = ?

Answer on page 22.

Ant facts

- Ant nests are often underground and have many tunnels.

- The queen ant is the biggest ant in the **colony**. She lays all the eggs.

- The worker ants in the colony are all female.

- Ants are one of the strongest creatures alive. They can lift up many times their own body weight!

Maths glossary

add to put groups of things together and find out how many in all

double to have twice as much of something

equals = This sign says equals. You use it to show the answer.

plus + This sign says plus. You use it to add one number to another number.

Ant glossary

anthill a mound made when ants dig their nest

colony a large group of something, such as ants

Index